W9-AXA-266

EDGE BOOKS™

NASCAR RACING

Behind the Wheel

by Matt Doeden

Consultant:
Suzanne Wise, Librarian
Stock Car Racing Collection, Belk Library
Appalachian State University
Boone, North Carolina

Capstone *press*®
Mankato, Minnesota

Edge Books are published by Capstone Press,
151 Good Counsel Drive, P.O. Box 669, Mankato, Minnesota 56002.
www.capstonepress.com

Library of Congress Cataloging-in-Publication Data
Doeden, Matt.
Behind the wheel / by Matt Doeden.
   p. cm.—(Edge books. NASCAR racing)
   Summary: "Describes what it's like to be a NASCAR driver, from pre-race
preparations to post-race activities"—Provided by publisher.
   Includes bibliographical references and index.
   ISBN–13: 978-1-4296-0084-2 (hardcover)
   ISBN–10: 1-4296-0084-5 (hardcover)
   1. NASCAR (Association)—Juvenile literature. 2. Stock car racing—Juvenile
literature. 3. Stock car drivers—Juvenile literature. I. Title.
GV1029.9.S74D634 2008
796.72—dc22   2007000250

Editorial Credits

Aaron Sautter, editor; Jason Knudson, set designer; Patrick D. Dentinger, book designer;
   Jo Miller, photo researcher

Photo Credits

AP/Wide World Photos/Joe Ranze, 6; Terry Renna, 26
Corbis/Craig Peterson/Icon SMI, 13; Dallas Morning News/Brad Loper, 22, Tom Fox, 19;
   GT Images/George Tiedemann, 20, 27, 28; Reuters/Pierre DuCharme, 7; The Sharpe
   Image/Sam Sharpe, 18; Worth Canoy/Icon SMI, cover; ZUMA/Robin Nelson, 25
The Sharpe Image/Sam Sharpe, 5, 9, 10, 14, 17

1 2 3 4 5 6 12 11 10 09 08 07

Table of Contents

CHAPTER 1

Running Up Front

The blue and white car roared down the front stretch of Daytona International Speedway. Only 14 laps remained in the 2006 Daytona 500. Jimmie Johnson was in second place in NASCAR's biggest race.

Johnson gripped the steering wheel tightly. It vibrated hard as he pushed his car to its limit. Traveling at nearly 200 miles (320 kilometers) per hour, Johnson focused on holding his position.

Johnson was only inches behind the leader, Brian Vickers. He decided to make a daring move. He dove down low on the track. Because he'd been drafting behind the leader, his car was just a little faster. Johnson pulled alongside Vickers and made the pass. He was in first place!

Jimmie Johnson (#48) worked hard to keep the lead in the 2006 Daytona 500.

Learn about:

→ The 2006 Daytona 500

→ Making bold moves

→ Holding onto the lead

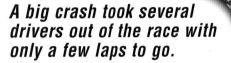

A big crash took several drivers out of the race with only a few laps to go.

In his rearview mirror, Johnson saw the other drivers fighting for position. Lines of cars were making bold moves to get ahead. But Johnson moved his car high and low on the track to block them.

With just three laps to go, a cloud of smoke appeared in Johnson's rearview mirror. His spotter told him there was an accident behind him. The flagman waved the yellow flag, signaling a caution. The drivers followed the pace car while officials cleared the track. It would be a three-lap shootout to victory.

Johnson led the pack at the restart. Behind him, he saw Casey Mears and Ryan Newman drafting. He knew that if they stayed together, they'd have a chance to pass him.

By the final lap, Mears still hadn't made his move. Newman tried to make the pass instead. But Mears stayed put, meaning Newman had no drafting partner. With two cars to pass and Johnson blocking the way, Newman couldn't get by. That's when Johnson knew he was going to win the Daytona 500! As he crossed the finish line, he shouted in victory. He had just scored one of the biggest wins of his career.

Johnson held onto the lead to win the race.

CHAPTER 2

The NASCAR Driver

NASCAR racing is a team sport. The crew chief, spotter, pit crew, and many others are all important. But no one has a bigger impact than the driver. Drivers need skill, patience, aggressiveness, and much more to succeed.

Preparing the Car

Many fans don't realize how much drivers do to get ready for a race. It's not as simple as just showing up and getting in the car. Drivers have many jobs to do before the green flag waves.

Ward Burton works with his team to prepare the car for each race.

Learn about:

➡ Testing the car and track
➡ Qualifying for the race
➡ Final adjustments

9

Ryan Newman and crew chief Matt Borland discuss strategies before each race.

A driver's most important job is helping the team prepare the car. Every NASCAR track is unique, and cars handle very differently at each one. Drivers make careful notes after each race. By studying how the car handles, teams can make the right adjustments. Drivers even help the team adjust the setup according to the weather forecast for race day.

Teams do lots of tests to get their cars set up just right for each race. Teams run some tests in the garage, but most of the fine-tuning happens on the track. Drivers take the car on practice runs to see how it handles. Then they tell their teams about problems that need to be fixed. Describing how the car handles during these tests is a huge part of the driver's job. A driver who can't tell the crew what's wrong won't win many races.

Race Weekend

Most NASCAR races are held on Sundays. Drivers must qualify on the Friday before the race. To qualify, drivers take turns on the track one by one. Each driver gets two laps to post the fastest possible time.

The starting order for Sunday's race is determined by each car's best time. Drivers need to perform at their best during the qualifying laps. Even a tiny mistake can mean starting the race deep in the field of 43 cars.

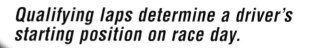
Qualifying laps determine a driver's starting position on race day.

After qualifying, drivers do several practice runs. They try out the different lanes to see where the car works the best. They run the car on the inside lane, the outside lane, and everywhere in between. Drivers also test their fuel mileage and see how the car handles on worn tires.

After practices, drivers work with their teams to make final adjustments before the race.

The most important practice comes on Saturday afternoon. This is the team's last chance to try out new setups and race strategies. The team then makes final pre-race adjustments to give the driver the best chance to win.

"Every race I go to is the most important race that we've got. And I prepare for every race the same way."
—Jeff Burton, NASCAR.com, 9/6/2006

CHAPTER 3

Race Day!

On race day, the team finds out if their hard work will pay off. For drivers, race day starts long before the green flag drops. They do interviews with TV, radio, and newspaper reporters. They meet with fans and sign autographs. They also work with their teams to make final preparations for the race.

Before every race, the drivers and crew chiefs meet with NASCAR officials. They review new race rules, dangers to avoid on the track, and any other concerns. Drivers then head to their teams' trailers. They dress in fireproof racing suits and review their racing strategy one last time.

Jimmie Johnson and other drivers often do interviews before each race.

Learn about:

➜ **Pre-race preparations**

➜ **Drafting strategies**

➜ **Post-race activities**

When the preparations are done, drivers put on their helmets and climb into their cars. Their crews help them strap in tightly. They're buckled in with harnesses and seat belts. Drivers' helmets are then hooked into a head restraint system called a HANS (Head And Neck Safety) device.

Drivers use lots of equipment to stay safe during a race.

When the green flag waves, drivers know it's time to compete for the prize.

Start Your Engines!

Once strapped in, the drivers wait for the most famous words in all of racing— "Gentlemen, start your engines!" After a few warm up laps, the race is on. Most races are about 500 miles (800 kilometers) long and last three to four hours.

Many drivers try to get an advantage by drafting and bumping other cars.

Drivers use all their skills to win a race. They try to draft, block, and bump their way to the front of the pack. They often drive aggressively, but they also know when to sit back and wait for their chance. NASCAR races are long. Drivers can't go full speed all the time. They know when to push it hard and when to ease back.

"I don't think what makes a good race car driver is a fearless person. I think it's somebody that is comfortable being behind the wheel of something that's somewhat out of control."

—Jeff Gordon, interview on *Larry King Live,* 2/23/2004

Drafting

During a race, drivers often follow just inches behind another car. This is called drafting. By running close together, two cars can lower the amount of air resistance they meet. Because they each push less air, they both can go a little bit faster.

Drafting is important on superspeedways like Daytona and Talladega. On these large tracks, drivers often go a step further. They use a strategy called bump drafting. These drivers don't just follow each other in a close line. They actually tap the car in front of them to get an extra boost.

Greg Biffle celebrates a big win with his team on victory lane.

After the Checkered Flag

With a lot of hard work and a little luck, a driver can take the checkered flag to win the race. But the day doesn't end there. After the race, drivers do more radio and TV interviews. The winner heads to victory lane to celebrate with the team.

Many drivers also meet with their sponsors after the race. These companies help pay the expenses of running the race team. Company sponsors usually have their name displayed somewhere on the race car. Drivers might do advertisements for their sponsors or just meet with company officials.

That evening or the next day, the driver and team carefully go over the race. They watch videos of the race and talk about what worked and what didn't. Drivers and teams then hurry to get to the next track. With a new race almost every week, there's little time to rest. They need to begin preparing for the next race.

CHAPTER 4

NASCAR Driving Greats

NASCAR is as much about the drivers as it is about cars and races. Great drivers are what make the sport fun and interesting. Legends like Richard Petty and current stars like Dale Earnhardt Jr. make racing fun for the fans.

Legends of the Past

Back in the 1950s, NASCAR relied on its biggest stars to draw a crowd. Buck Baker, Lee Petty, and Bud Moore made the sport popular. But NASCAR's first true superstar arrived in the early 1960s.

Richard Petty is the most successful driver in NASCAR history. In his career, he won 200 Cup races and seven championships. During the 1967 season, Petty won 27 of the season's 49 Cup races. He even won a record 10 in a row. With records like that, Petty really earned his nickname, "The King."

Richard Petty is a legend among NASCAR drivers.

Learn about:

→ "The King"

→ "The Intimidator"

→ Today's stars

"The King" remained popular through the 1970s. But soon, a new star appeared. With his bold driving style, Dale Earnhardt Sr. quickly earned the nickname, "The Intimidator." Earnhardt was never afraid to bump another car out of his way. His style worked well. Earnhardt won seven Cup titles before he was killed in a crash at the 2001 Daytona 500.

"Dale Earnhardt was the greatest race car driver that ever lived. He could do things with a race car that no one else could."
—Former Cup champion Ned Jarrett, after Dale Earnhardt Sr's death in the 2001 Daytona 500

Dale Earnhardt Sr. was NASCAR's biggest star during the 1980s and 1990s.

Like his father, Dale Earnhardt Jr. has become one of NASCAR's biggest stars.

Today's Greats

Today, NASCAR has many stars. One of the sport's most popular drivers is Dale Earnhardt Jr. But Junior, as most people call him, hasn't relied on his father's famous name. He's become a star on his own. Junior has won two Busch Series titles and has been in the hunt for several Cup championships. Junior is also famous for his skills on NASCAR's biggest tracks, especially Talladega Superspeedway.

Jeff Gordon is the most successful NASCAR driver racing today.

Jeff Gordon burst onto the NASCAR scene in the early 1990s. He soon became one of NASCAR's top drivers. He won four championships in his first nine seasons. Gordon is known for his skill on short tracks and road courses. But he's a threat to win on any track. NASCAR fans always know where his rainbow-colored #24 car is.

Dozens of stars fill today's NASCAR ranks. There is always someone to root for or against. People don't just watch NASCAR races to see the cars. They also love to watch and cheer for their favorite NASCAR drivers.

NASCAR Greats

Name	Years	Wins	Championships
Bobby Allison	1961, 1965–1988	85	1
Dale Earnhardt Jr.	1999–	17	0
Dale Earnhardt Sr.	1975–2001	76	7
Jeff Gordon	1992–	75	4
Jimmie Johnson	2001–	26	1
David Pearson	1960–1986	105	3
Richard Petty	1958–1992	200	7
Tony Stewart	1999–	29	2
Rusty Wallace	1980–2005	55	1
Darrell Waltrip	1972–2000	84	3
Cale Yarborough	1957, 1959–1988	83	3

Glossary

caution (KAW-shuhn)—a time during a race when the drivers have to slow down and are not allowed to pass; a caution occurs after a crash or when the track crew has to clean up debris.

crew chief (KROO CHEEF)—the member of a race team in charge of the car and the crew; the crew chief helps the driver choose racing strategies.

HANS device (HANZ de-VISSE)—a system of straps that holds a driver's head in place in case of a wreck

qualify (KWAHL-uh-fye)—to earn a starting spot in a race by completing timed laps

road course (ROHD KORSS)—a track that has many right and left turns and only a few short straightaways

sponsor (SPON-sur)—a person or company that pays a race team to put advertisements on the car

spotter (SPAH-tuhr)—a team member who sits high above the track and tells the driver where other cars are on the track

superspeedway (SOO-pur-speed-way)—a large race track that is more than 1.5 miles (2.4 kilometers) long, with an oval shape and high banked turns

Read More

Buckley, James Jr. *NASCAR: Speedway Superstars.*
Pleasantville, N.Y.: Reader's Digest, 2004.

Schaefer, A. R. *Dale Earnhardt Jr.* NASCAR
Racing. Mankato, Minn.: Capstone Press, 2005.

Woods, Bob. *Earning a Ride: How to Become a
NASCAR Driver.* The World of NASCAR. Maple
Plain, Minn.: Tradition Books, 2004.

Internet Sites

FactHound offers a safe, fun way to find Internet
sites related to this book. All of the sites on FactHound
have been researched by our staff.

Here's how:

1. Visit *www.facthound.com*

2. Choose your grade level.

3. Type in this book ID **1429600845** for age-appropriate sites.
   You may also browse subjects by clicking on letters, or by
   clicking on pictures and words.

4. Click on the **Fetch It** button.

FactHound will fetch the best sites for you!

Index